More Ways Than One

A collection of poems: Few to soothe and
Far to brood

Aritra Kumar Das

BookLeaf
Publishing

India | USA | UK

Made with ❤ on the BookLeaf Publishing Platform
www.bookleafpub.in
www.bookleafpub.com

Dedication

To

The One who Believed that I can

Fly

My first and foremost teacher

My Guru, My Master - My

Father.

Preface

Have you ever felt like you need someone to lend you an ear but without condescension or judgement in their gaze? Not just a friend who'll be there during your fun banters or an experienced but distanced therapist, but someone who you can trust your thoughts, your mind(s) with? Well, these poems were that for me and I trust they can do the same for you. They will listen to you. They will. This is the best thing about these poems, they don't just narrate, but they can listen as well. I don't have the temerity to say that these are all brilliant works of art. That's for you to decide. But one thing that I do know for sure is that, they'll be there for you, whenever you need them. Through your moments of high and low, through those cosily dull days of monsoon or achingly eventful days of spring or summer, through those new bonds and old heartbreaks - they'll be there to accompany you. That's what they are, your companions. Hope you wouldn't desert them, and being with them for so long, I can reassure you, they never would.

Acknowledgements

This book, at least the way it appears to be, would never have seen the light of day without the tremendous contributions of several people - the first and foremost among them being, my parents. My father, Dr. Anup Kumar Das, is an erudite man and a better poet than I ever could be, and it was he who inspired me to pick up the pen. My mother, Mrs. Jayashri Das, is genuinely one of the most artistic ladies that I've ever seen in my life, her lens had always been an extremely interesting one. She taught me, to be able to perceive in more ways than one. My brother, Mr. Amartya Kumar Das, a post-graduate in English Literature and a masterful literary critic himself, gave me the necessary exposure and context to navigate the seemingly boundless realm of English literature and provided me with advice that only a literary scholar can. It was his appreciation and nurturing that gave me wings. And last in the segment, but certainly not the least, my partner-in-crime, Ms. Bingshati Sarkar, who had been my muse in several instances and in varied manners, weaving such intricate experiences and memories for me, that it shaped me into the person I am today.

They have always been here to support me, no matter the circumstances. And they're the reason that I can dare to take the plunge. Thank you for your unconditional love and support.

My friends, colleagues and all those who comprise of my extended family have been with me every step of the way, sharing their feedbacks and cheering me through the entire duration of the race. They've been extremely supportive of me. If I have to name a few, my colleague and dear friend, Mr. Abhijit Mandal, my senior colleague Ms. Arpita Chowdhury who had been like an elder sister to me and the erudite Principal of my School, a man of letters himself, Mr. Umesh Kumar deserves special mention. My students have also been a constant source of inspiration for me, their variety, their depth and my interactions with them, added inexplicable flavours to my work.

A big shoutout to the impeccable team at Book Leaf Publishing who've been with me throughout the journey, without whom this book, would've remained an unrealized dream forever.

And my heartfelt gratitude and apologies to all those who I couldn't name here, but, whose kind words have helped me finish this project, the way I wanted to.

1. PARAFFIN HEART

We live in someone's heaven, or is my hell just lost to
you ?
Light gleams off the wax, or is my skin just breaking
through!

If someone starts a fire, my paraffin heart, skips a beat;
What lights every desire, serves me - infernal heat ...

I'd had a broken neck, my nadir's always held my gaze:
Tried to navigate through, reflections in a shimmering
haze.

I try to grow, but beat my brow and, always end up
riverside,
The evening breeze don't flush my soul, end up clenching
my raw hide.

Gaping wounds and claxons boom, as I get through my
demon days,
Last of us had me forlorn, bloating whales and crowded

bays.

Dream of being baptized to life, but had been, tantalized
before,
Want to share this sunset with, someone, at this silent
shore.

I find my bleeding feet somewhere and start to screw the
hex bolts in,
Careful, as to not spark yet, my heart's still full of
paraffin.

2. En sång från huvudstaden

Been ages since my soles have felt the solace in a verdant
plush,

'been ages since my face has faced something that's not
assault.

My heart is, aflutter since, it does not heed my eager
hush

My consciousness, is ensconced, in a breathless state of
halt.

The maggots never abandon me, they're seated deep
inside my flesh

The only way I know to be free - matches & timber
stacked afresh.

I was alive, like mold thrives, on rancid, putrefying mass

Why'd you wash me in sun & breeze, in the midst of
decaying carcass ?

Your music haunts me, birdsong taunts me, the frozen
blood will start to thaw...

And like an echo of bygone era, the pain of life will start
to gnaw.

Let me get back to my Lethe abode, blanketed in moss,
it's far below,

A place where I got to feel at home, where winter burns
and summers snow.

*(The title of this poem simply means 'A Song from the
Capital', in Swedish. I leave the rest to you, to uncover
what it truly implies and to evaluate, if it succeeds in
doing so.)*

3. RIDESHARE

The mind in me has a mind of its own
It seldom listens to what I don't say
Like a kettle-full corn, that's left too long
It pops too fowl, smelling of burnt hay

I wake up good with a halo on my head
A Samaritan soul that nurses all ill
But before the sun's on a downward arc
I change, I rage, I'm raring to kill...

On a stroll, I look at the hearts holding hands
A wistful tear wells up in my eye
The very next day I burn the dried roses
The darling - gleaming. How can I defy ?

Like a long rolled up paper, that stubbornly flips
I clip my wings as soon as they grow
My flight's like a fall, like a string-less doll
I freeze up to a wall. Next hour ? I flow.

My heart, it beats on an awful whimsy
Racing through the sands and still like a stone
But, my blood carries all my untold guilt
Maybe blended raw, like a shaman's drone

Each time I sleep, I fear she'll wake
My twin, my bane, my vengeful other
A smile on my face and a tear in my heart
This passenger rides like, there ain't another ...

4. BIOGRAPHY

Two steps forward and one to the side
It's mostly in your loss that I can thrive
The needle never works, to the left, to the right.

Two to the side and one step forward
There's only ever one, mine against your word.

Two steps backward and one to the side
My soul's long left this mortal device
Adorned with oaths, is the body of my lies.

Two to the side and one step backward
I'm out of your way; lurking in the backyard.

Two steps forward and one to the side
I slash through cords to create divides
My marionettes see strings, still take their dives

Two to the side and one step forward
Muted the Themis, had Phthisis honoured

I leap over the pawns, whether mine or yours
As a statesman I know, to win you endure
My ledger is as checkered, as the ground that I tread
Falling off the race - is the only thing I dread
I have my monarch and his queen to serve
Yet when it suits me, I'm the first one to swerve
I wear a shining armour, maybe I'm what you think
Not state, code or praise; it's your blood that I drink.

5. SIESTA SOLILOQUY

Gunpowder and roses, 'trade both with swift dispatch

Burns and lead kisses ... I treat at random, out of batch

The smell of blood hangs heavy in air, everyday at 4 o'
clock

Whether of burns from lead or lips, questions ringing
block by block

Everyday at 4 PM, the blades call out for want of blood

Serenaded by feathery dust, my symphony feeds on
raging flood

Walk a mile, swim some more and once you get to catch
your breath

A single question reigns supreme, stench of love or
strength of death

The elevation, my pedestal, the one which I may goad
about

Does it comprise of dried blood or mix of iron ? Still
some doubt...

As soon as the breeze becomes stiff, my 4 PM guests
shall all arrive

Even if my ferry capsizes fast, those ceaseless hands will

start to thrive.
So, I don't care for medicine man, my burning heart's past septic phase
All I want is a final toll, that stops the 4 o'clock goose chase.

6. MY CONFESSIONS

It doesn't hurt that bad, the wounds have healed a long time ago now.

I've resumed my therapy, again, and it does feel better, to be candid.

I've learnt to look at metamorphosis and got the reason why pain works and how.

Honestly, I still enjoy the sweet relief of midday petrichor and bliss at the dusk of dawn.

The birdsongs must be nice, maybe the carnival too;

And if they vouch for the delectable ecstasies maybe

Maybe they're reassuringly true

But the problem with a broken clock is simple, the feigning can only work twice

What good does it do to fortify the mind, if the heart has
lost all its spine ?

I still wake up, want to hum a melody, want to wait for
you as we grow old...

But the urge to let them rest is stronger than ever,
Doesn't help the accused that they'd been peeled raw
I want them to raise the dragonslayer,
But they seem to be under the shade of the Night - My
shoulders...

And the urge to let them rest is much stronger, manifold.

There's not much abuse or deep seated trauma, I think

No potion for sleepy lucidity in what I drink

But the weight of the resounding vacuum that grows
heavier each time

Each time I stop to negotiate or to blink...

My petrified shoulders watch in horror,

As the ivories get a fresh coat of ink...

No sinister serpent uncoils itself in my deepest recess

There's no lake of fire or demented waters

That scare me.

The sweet relief from this nausea, that the repetitive
undulations had brought on;

If I indulge, my road to perdition awaits me

Let the sepulchre of normalcy and normalisation be
undisturbed.

I'm not gonna go for any violent atonement at all,

It's going to be a leisurely and welcoming stroll

With a much awaited friend of mine, one bound to me
by his oath.

A walk across the park and off to a safe place, safe from,
All the weight, the weights of indecisions and waits:
That peeled the skin off my shoulder, there will be
remedy for that too.

After I have stopped the wheel of time,
The one that's always beating my drum.

7. AN ODE TO VACUUM

You're raw,
Flayed, so very naked...
Yet there's no spectrum
Not even a hint
When...
Light passes through you.

Your bones, your teeth and your dwindling spine
Is for everyone to see
They're so featureless.
So smooth that,
Light gleams off across the ends
Of your bones...

Absurdly large holes
Where your ears were supposed to be
Are you still trying to trap
Reverberating echoes ?
Like the shrewd king's relentless boulder,
You haven't changed, even in your demise...

Oh dear, you can't ! Can you ?

The hollow of your eyes are so very striking
Did someone pluck them out for you ?
Over and over again ?
So that you don't have to blink
When you lie ?
Not for nothing, in vain...

Have you ever likened yourself
To the fancy
Of a beautiful man
Draped in yellow and white
Admiring his shimmering semblance ?

Have you just been that much?
Was your contention not interrupted
By the glow of your neighbour's glamour ?

Can you sleep well?
Can your screaming void
Manifest itself
Into functional eyelids ?
Can you ever close them ?
To sleep, maybe for a few hours ...

I asked a raven to guide your soul
But he came back soon,
Untainted, his view still sharp
He couldn't find it...

I hope you can.

Maybe you won't be so terribly disfigured the next time.
Maybe you won't need some foreigner to gently place a
dime,

Upon your still eyes,
The next time.

8. THE LAST SONG FROM THE CAVES OF GIBRALTAR

A gentle breeze goes kissing my cheeks
And teases my eyelids firmly shut
An afternoon reverie is all I get
As my nest might wake up...
If not in a rut.

I roam amidst the damp and cold
Rough rocks beneath my sole
I step and slip and fall on them
My feet don't hurt -
They're coal.

My face wasn't this in another
life, with eyes such sapphire green !
I can't recall, just how I looked
Was I plump and pink...
Or thin ?

All that slithers in my nest now
They bite, they tear and burn,
I don't know how I look anymore
Not a beauteous one -
Down turn.

My face - it burns and stings sometimes
Well, times that I can't see
But I can't feel a tinge of warmth
On my flesh, my face -
To be.

My ravenous wards, the ones I
nurse, 'cause I can't - them
Forsake...
Their venom rushes through my bones
And brings my heart
At stake...

Can't scratch my head, it hurts them
Babes, the raging den of gall
But, I still fear if I add...
Another, yet other flesh
To this pall.

I can't help it, but I wanted to

It pleased me for a time;
Now I dread, any footsteps in
My cairn, to add to the
Water of rime.

I don't know where my sisters are
I can't remember their names
All I see, from my childhood days
Are our titters, at our -
Silly games.

Well, it's time, I better get back
That's breeze enough for the dead
Can't let a tranquil moment of peace
Just get up to...
My head.

9. FINALITY

Drip-drip-drop, it comes to a stop
A thousand steps and billions drop
I feel those anchors weighing at me,
Receding now, as I turn around
I feel the sundials damaged now,
Prickly pins - all left at the ground.

Drop-drop-drip, the price seems steep
Yet you'll pay, no shelter to keep -
To keep you from the ripple effect
Come look at me, I'm naked now,
My teeth, my nails all bloodstained - sharp
I'll sink them again, as per my vow.

Drip-drip-drop, I would love to hop
No playground now, but on your top -
The top you've carved so carefully
From my meat, my beat, my ecstasy
Might keep your throne, might burn it down
The details will follow -- in my testacy.

Drop-drop-drip, my blood you'll keep
And let it settle or let it seep...
It will seep, all' way, down to your soul
To remind of my deaths, my rapes, my all
You'll learn soon, how tears can smell
How it feels to be broken, long before you fall...

Drop by drop, I will reclaim,
What I am owed, all in my name
The tears, the pangs, the lashes of hunger
The lack of all - of dreams, of life
Here I come, with metal in my breath
Here I come, raining death on your bunker...

And once the debt is paid in full
My hair is clean, the moon is cool
The sun will rise - a gleeful warm
The birds will sing, with us in arms...
I'll teach my kid, there's no such thing
No men or women - just human being

10. DISCOVERY

I had been lying dead, motionless like a cairn forsaken
There were no undulations neither any chaos in me,
I hadn't known any promises, nor any oaths have been
taken –
I had a complete reign in this vast void, yet I was hardly
free.

No bells tolled, nor an ominous dispatch received
Oracles were yet to be born, granular silence reigned;
I had never thought that my absolution could be
deceived
My aridity upturned, the unfarmed terrains have rained

Abruptly, I felt a lilting melody echo through my chasm:
Slowly it grew intense, accompanied by a scent –
I felt a pulse growing steady into an acute spasm
Almost too painful, didn't stop at the uncharted ascent!

No squalls, not raving madness, it was but-
Another pulse, a rhythm that synced to my person

It grew closer and drew me to its beating heart
Metal and dust aloof, it was a sincere sermon,

It called out to me, you called and I felt a million pangs
Life unfurled itself to be a cruel mist, obstructing the
view
It came all drenched in sweat, striking the iron walls
with cosmic bang
You birthed the primordial spark in me, it branched into
countless hues.

I was like sand before being touched by your love
I could build makeshift castles, only to be washed
offshore
Now that I've been kissed by your fire roaring up and
above
I'm definite and brittle like glass, but I could be
ephemeral and more.

You have mothered twice, once myself; then our streams
Conjoined, they took on all our dances and tales and
colours and notes;
Made musical paintings with broken moonbeams –
Willed wild outgrowths into reality, protected them with
their garrisoned forts.

Is it time to heal the gashes, fall back onto the dark

embrace ?
Would you believe I'd already checked, latent, deep at
dusk ?
Neither your home could be found nor my prenatal
address!
Instead, I uncovered a fibrous womb, slimed up like a
conspicuous cusk.

It sang soft lullabies with oh so peaceful sounds of storm
We could stay there until our next act or forevermore
Either way, I get to travel your recess in your form
We will erupt into chaos and want and everlasting lore.

11. MY VOWS

I have waited an eternity and pondered over another
Whether I can endure or fail my dear mother,
My wick ne'er lit on its own, nor did my gospels sing
All my life I've lived in meadows, but ne'er did the
church bells ring.

Then, by chance, you came and lit a big blue flame
You let the music echo through the valley, whispering
our names.
I grew a feet higher, now reaching for the shooting stars-
Gone were the days when, I had to, admire them from
afar,

You gave me song and sunshine, filled my colour palette
And taught me how to forge a life using a golden mallet
We flew together, danced in rain and plunged the depths
all day
I made a promise I'll ne'er rush, or push you, come what
may.

And now that I can hear, the music at the end of line
Waves of chill, quite far from thrill, shivers through my
spine
My nights have grown weary, I fear, if I'll keep my word
This quiet betrays disquiet in mind, if I choose to hurt,

Stones unturned and songs unheard, flights we'd ne'er
flown,
I want to have them all one day before we've both
outgrown
I've promised to give you all I have, but this I'll never
share
My shrinking heart will heal itself, when I'll smell your
hair

So, I revow to stand my ground and wait for you my love
The lighthouse shall be unabandoned with beacon up
above
I'll root my feet in warm baywater and listen to birds
returning
But most of all, I swear to you, I'll ne'er once leave us
burning.

12. ROUTINE

Have you seen how
The rain washes away the must
How the warm rays of sun
Clean it up nice and smooth
How this corner becomes new
Bathed in the radiance and
Illuminated in the crisp downpour ?

Only to be covered in
Mildew, afresh and
just
When you thought that
They're not to come, to invade again
But they still arrive, at the
Table to enjoy the succour...

Have you heard his screams ?
When the giant bird
Ripped apart his guts and ate away,
At his liver, bit

By bit, every single day,
And still flew back next day
To eat some more ?

Or, have you also ventured
Through the dark and
Cold desolation
Of the realm where our love
Our satin liquid love is
Harvested and locked away
In strange looking jars

After you've had your limbs
Tired and tried
But also slightly jubilant
With the coveted prize
Only to be called back by
A siren song that draws
You in and replaces your
Reward with scars ?

Have you ever smelled like
The strange scent of
Rock fuel from
beneath
That some cherish and yet
Others despise

Have you felt the need
To dive deep into
This maddening chaos
And sort everything out
By your own
To revise ?

I can't remember how I smelled
Felt or dreamed
My skin is much too smooth
To the point of
Incandescence
All I know is that I've got to go back
Account for once more
Decorate everything one
Last time.
Before I meet my
Demise...

13. REVERBERANT

The times come back, fingers wrapped in...
The memories of quaint, rings over the din-
Footsteps
On the mountain path
Transcending the lore of men,
Longing sighs and longing glance
Sweating up the lonesome pane;
Dust to dust, even diamonds rust...
What stays alive is quest of fools,
The books you love, your music feed
Keeps coming back, and back......
Indeed.

14. ALREADY

A spider, an elephant and a peahen
Devourer, a leader and adherent.
I've been reflected countless times,
In works of art or useless rhymes.
I've been admired, loved or killed
Peals of laughter or tears filled.
I've nourished and groomed
Left broken and doomed
I've also made the rivers flow
Witnessed winters thaw in glow
Life burst forth from frozen womb
I have had enshrined my past in tomb.
Infernal pain that clutches your soul
I've swallowed that and marched to the goal.
There's ceiling shards beneath your feet
A beating heart beneath my meat.

What more do I need to accomplish?
How far shall I draw the line ?
Who cares for your Excalibur?

I've already been divine.
I've already been through all ordeals
Already crafted so many seals
That prove my bonafide, my mettle
I've waited until your wound heals.
Now my tether's tattered rough,
You better brace for a close impact
And karma's not gonna forgive, though
I know, I'm standing by its trestle.

15. RENDEZVOUS

There was an air - warm with ecstasy,
Born out of the warmth of an even warmer embrace
It swirled around, high above the ground
Jubilant, deeply lost in itself and proud...

It came across another - bereft of all life
The spring blossoms dreaded it - such cold was its touch
It didn't smell of longing, neither had lament felt like its
sound...
But it could define the very meaning of lonesome - even
in a crowd.

The first one tried to bring its elder back to the fold
Out of its blithering reality of what seemed to birth cold
It said with a warm laughter that filled the whole room
up with a flutter
'No sorrow ever was worth it, your joy, your life, what
could be - without all the clutter.'

The second one was older, much slower, rusty from its

dives across the rail yard;
It smelled of duckweed and stale goodbyes from across
the stations, quite like the cards...
It flashed an eerie smile, one laced with the inevitability
of knowing
It said, "Son, the compass ain't broken, my heart is - but I
still know where I'm going."

16. REIMAGINING

Almost motionless, save for lullaby
Hunchback tamarind, it's verdant blinking canopy
Tasted my tears here, revelled in the laugh
Louder than the boom of rapids, echoing through the
trough

Petrichor, send me home
I've been chained, to these roads
Crusty footsteps, rusty breath
Petrichor, take me home...

I've been waiting, almost too far away
As I keep fading, with each passing day
Wayward and waylaid, keep all spirits chained
Can't find my address, a tattered old hag, my friend...

Petrichor, send me home
I've been chained, to these roads
Crusty footsteps, rusty breath

Petrichor, take me home...

I fear if I get back maybe I won't know the last straw
Grayscale does remind me of my tethers far away
(Waitin') by my shadow, think I'd a reckonin'
My address had been wrong since a fateful yesterday,
yesterday...

Petrichor, send me home
I've been chained, to these roads
Crusty footsteps, rusty breath
Petrichor, take me home...

Petrichor, send me home
I've been chained, to these roads
Crusty footsteps, rusty breath
Petrichor, take me home...

Take me home, St. Petrichor
Take me home, St. Petrichor

*(This was a tribute to a favourite song of my mine, I
believe you know by now which one I'm talking about.
It's a personal favourite of mine and this is nothing but a
humble way - my humble way, of honouring the legend -
John Denver.)*

17. BEFORE I LEAVE

I'll be back, once the dust settles
When the skies are blue again
Now it's time - the stubborn skittles
They need to know, the meaning of pain.

Don't worry now, I'll be alright
I promise, I'll keep my light alive
'cause it's a long party, it ain't a fight
They won't do well where lilies don't thrive.

I've got a job, it's just the one
Stay in line and stick to the plan
The rusty stain - on the tip of my gun
Not mine, it comes from the enemies' clan.

I'll be grinning from ear to ear
When I get back home and kiss your cheek
Ma, I'll be cleaning, the world of its fear
Got to make sure, it doesn't run too thick.

Bonnie, won't you wait ? Just two short summers...
I can't sleep well, if you can't be proud;
The way you sang and the drone of these hummers
Incessant and stark, but stills a lot of crowd.

18. TIPTOE

The glare of the Sun is a dagger in my eye
On a whim, if my glance, does a moment linger
Equally true, does guide a lantern fly
Without the need to press on a hurting finger.
My eyes seek you, my ears seek your laugh
My prayers and thoughts are all saturated
In pain your touch, as a parched horse, to the trough
Like pearls to the thread, my worship's uncomplicated.

My tears and my blood, they're mortal designs
But they're worth their salt, when flowing in your name.
My heart doesn't beat - that's the only science;
It's a Motown Groove, playing through, an old ball game.
If I come clean to you with all I've been feeling -
I fear your reply will be calling off the game,
Can't reign in my heart, as its walls are a peelin'
The last time I sing, it's gonna be your name.

19. CLEARANCE MAIL

Dear You, now you walk 'nother ground
I know not if it's wet or dry
The silence screams such mighty loud
Shattering all, beyond the cry.

At each turn of your lovelorn house
Feels, a glimpse shall now be caught
Flaming lamps, I had them doused
The hope rings strong, but it was naught.

I dream of barters, fair or not
An audience with you, one last time
To tell you how I dearly sought
To swap the names, in lists for a dime.

As I walk through the dog-eared pages
Or neat little folds in books of yours
Feels like the rattling old cages
Tend to turn like they did before.

Your mayflower garden's now wasting
Matters not whether I plant or plough
To take them where you're resting
To tell them all, I don't know how.

Through Oblivion – and all its mist
You grabbed the one succinct
Rest easy, surely, put down your list
Step out of your own precinct.

As the flesh of a fresh fruit ripens, and
The bulk of it falls on the ground
Blocked the ticker's flow, and the sand
You stopped the wheel, its turnaround.

As soon as you left, and I was bereft
Voices green with venom's sting
Opened rifts & took me to the cleft
And hammered 'cross my battered being.

You left like a spinner does its weave
I can't see you – but your stubborn prints
I'll never ask why you had to leave
Maybe leave me on this wayward crimp.

Beyond the grip of Earth's succour
Or other forms of mortal woes,

Your shuttle of dreams in all splendour
Where to go ? It does surely know.

Roam across the vast time lane
And all extremes of space as well
If you ever need to get back home,
I'll always be there, in my hale.

(This poem was composed as an elegy for someone very dear to me, but it has been composed from a perspective that's not mine, but one that belongs to her daughter. I don't know if it can reach the departed, but I sure wish it does.)

20. BALLAD OF A CHAOTIC DRUMBEAT

A draught-free, sightless, endless sea
Devoid of clutter, devoid of pain
Seems as lifeless as I can be
Devoid of scowls with utter disdain

A hum emanates and grows to a boom –
The hummer doesn't gleam, it's incognito.
A darkness groans in its birthing room
A feint of a croon, is it my base retort ?

Minutes ripple up as young seconds grow
As waves part, pearls grin; sands take shape_
Like buffering winds in a hammer throw
Sound through this silence – I can't escape...

Supple fireballs through a queer growth phase
It's time, they will it – to really come alive.
Two ones make a two, a million you blazes
Hums start to drum up as the orbs now thrive –

Once they're aglow, the dust starts to flow_
Trace a path 'long a wandering conic
With the beats of the drum, the warmth starts to grow;
Unwavering eccentric, a waning unique

As the fireballs shine, like a unique design
Dust births elements to pierce through the soil
The dewed leaf glistens, a glorious divine
Beats become breath, surveilled by 'the foil':

Fins start to ripple, and the trampling hooves
The fishbowl pair grows caverns to sniff
With antlers and tails and evergrowing grooves
Lone angels rejoice at 'nother hummer's whiff

As the neck grows short, with horizon in sight
The hummer, drummer, flautist – they stop, she stops
Thoughts turn to music, now that thumbs can fight
The angels now dance, they drown when she drops...

I've been a mute, a witness till date,
My breast longed the touch as the drumming gnaws
I know you might be sore, but it's a fickle fate
Whimper at my chest, I'll comb you as it snows

... And, I'll comb you...

As it snows...

21. MIRAGE?

Far from the exuberant crowd
From well-wishers, soothsayers, my friends and-
Family...
Alone in this desolate, dark and frigid dust
Never out of breath or pace.

I am to be the beacon,
To keep roving
As the will-o'-the-wisp does
Over a brooding marsh.

To know.

I am to be the beacon,
To keep looking
As a starving mongrel does
Through a bursting bin.

To know.

I am to be the beacon,
To keep thinking
As a distraught father
Over his only son.

To know.

I am to be eternal,
To stay by my lonesome
Talk to myself;
And write to my family.

Forever and beyond.

To know.

(This was composed the day man successfully landed a lunar module for the very fist time at the South Pole of Moon. It's been composed from the perspective of Pragyan, the lunar rover and all its kin, eternal wanderers on alien soil.)

22. INTO THE DOLDRUMS

A splendid sea, so beautiful, it takes your breath away
Cast into it, with fluttering sails, my ship's now led
astray
This vast expanse, a void azure, the lay of a landless land.
A timeless toll, a fateless fate, a senseless guiding hand.

As I gasped for a breath or two, in this calm seascape
The dead weight on my lungs, fish out acid free tape
Something to mend my lean soul with, to hide the
gaping cracks;
The bigger the glass, the more it runs, the faster it could
track.

As my smoky breath shoots, goes on to touch the roof
Born in my lungs and borne by the air, squeezed out
aloof.
So do the dark thoughts grow, towering upon the first
Despair to death and careful breath, feeding the flames of
thirst...

As I pace through aimless paths, inch by inch and day by
day,
Sure as rain, bright as dusk, my reaching eyes can no
more play
This voyage is a means to an end, though end seems
farther off
The more I stay, the more I play, the stakes don't rise,
they drop.

As I amble fore to aft, in calm of blue, I step steady
I feel the motion's stopped beneath, even if you're not
ready
A timeless toll, a fateless fate, a senseless guiding hand.
This vast expanse, a void azure, the lay of a landless land.

23. ACID RAIN

Pit-pat from above, drips all day
Pattering stops not, come what may
I feel so cold and violated
Cry as I want, they still want to 'play'...

At night, in dreams, they still invade
I bleed or weep, but it pervades
I feel fractured, I can't be whole
Can't heal, I will - incinerate

The last traces of , what's my soul
Shatters forth as lead through the goal
Like sly raindrop that wets your all
Wounds burn through me like burning coal

Betrayed by kin, Goliaths do fall
With bloodied lips and heart of gall -
My suffering casts infernal pall
These sufferings cast infernal pall.

24. EXPIRATION

A little of she, a little of me...
And a lot of what wasn't, in between.
From dollars to dime,
A little of time...
And 'we' were never seen.

A little to flee, a little too free...
Not a lot of any was all around
'neath flaking lime,
Got our list of crimes...
And 'we' could never again be found.

25. ALUMNI

I went out for a walk
Down by the babbling brook
Beyond the insane spring
It's every cranny and nook
Was covered in a mist
Like liberty, did it look.

I went out for a stroll
'cross the highland plains
Between the crashing knots
Out back - my capital gains
It indeed was a war
Where all but one was slain.

I went out for a jaunt
Up to the valley of rose
It smelled like sweetened milk
Like pleasure, straight through nose.
Wonder what went down
Before your justice posed.

Round I went for a mooch
Through this morning breeze
Where poets never sang
Or cracked upon a tease
Where bells and chalk dust lie
In eternal freeze.

26. DESERT BLOOM

Roses bloom all over the vale

Mountains, rivers and by the dale...

But the ones in desert soak all the sun

And become the most glorious one.

Not for their colour, nor their savour,

For me the thorns did do outdone.

27. SUMMER RETREAT

I used to love the summer months
When scorching heat hid tons of rain
As monsoons came to drench me through
The pinpricked skin had much to drain

My childhood summers had succulent treats
Jasmine blossoms and balsam bees
The radiant sun had a fatherly scowl
The cooling shade of milkwood trees

As the first raindrops touched parched mud lips
A heavenly smell hung heavy in air
Like a passionate kiss from lover's reunion
That liquid love crept through my hair

I heard them streams and ponds and lakes
Their happy lungs warbling high melody
I've seen two toddy palms bathe in rain
As one blushed and turned in chastity

The summer penance of dried mire
Melted in a countless shower arms
The torrid breath of afternoons
Replaced with evening moans in the farm

I seem to have lost those monsoon days,
Can't find them in my trophies' stack
What happened to those grinning Mays ?
Where those lovers are when I gaze out back ?

What seem to rule these sanitary days
Are visors, masks and pill caddy
Like chanting children of Chernobyl
Who ain't ever gonna meet Daddy.

28. WILL-O'-THE-WISP

Whistling wisps of whimper now
Are all I can manage anyhow
Tremors at the base of my throat
Are trapped in a net, laid out on a boat.
I want to scream or sing a rhyme
Yet fail myself, just everytime

My songs have left me, speeches too
Confessions crashed in countless hues
Wanted to say, how I love you
Now that seems like a fading blue
Cryptic thrums of horror kills
And redrum filled with daffodils

My words are leaving; free from me
Chipping away at my sanity
I won't be whistling tunes or a hum
I'll be quiet, as a tarpit drum.
From olive orchard to sunset shore
My laughter won't be heard anymore.

I will not scream or sing a rhyme
Won't fail myself, just everytime
No tremors at the base of throat
Are trapped in a net, laid out on a boat.
Whistling wisps of whimper now
Are all I can manage anyhow.

29. AN 18-HOUR YEAR

A burning world so fixated
It burns through eternal time
As years collapse to under a day
It plays infernal rime

It likes kisses that sears its flesh
And bathes a thousand wounds
It follows a heartless master now
Inflicting a million runes

It's rocky heart gets burnt to ash
And strewn across the sky
Covered in streams of molten rage
Even death does not pass by

Rage over a week, a raging month
Now rage has lost its kin
A fiery pit of pent-up rage
Let's count each other's sins.

30. A MIRRORED FLIGHT

A fluttering thing just flew past me
A riot of black, red, white
Its wings were a sizzled sienna hue
Black crown refined right.

It sang a song I've often heard
Melodic rhythm and blue
And with its dainty steps the bird
Had made me a hoofer too

I prepped a golden cage for it
Adorned with a bonsai fig
Amused it circled over me
And chortled at my gig

I paused and glanced with asking gaze
And doubtless was its coo
'Am I the captive you want
Or in there, it's just you ?'

www.ingramcontent.com/pod-product-compliance
Lightning Source LLC
Chambersburg PA
CBHW061711130726
47996CB00006B/2261